Original title:
Starlit Chill

Copyright © 2024 Swan Charm
All rights reserved.

Author: Johan Kirsipuu
ISBN HARDBACK: 978-9916-79-654-2
ISBN PAPERBACK: 978-9916-79-655-9
ISBN EBOOK: 978-9916-79-656-6

Polished Gussets of Aether

In twilight's glow, the stars align,
Whispers of dreams in shadows pine.
The moon's soft touch, a silken thread,
Guiding us where the heart is led.

A tapestry wove in silver light,
Lifting the veil from the night.
Echoes flutter in the gentle breeze,
Moments captured, like autumn leaves.

Through polished gussets, time flows free,
A dance of souls, a symphony.
Each heartbeat mirrors the cosmic song,
Binding us where we all belong.

In realms unseen, where spirits play,
The essence lingers, night and day.
A canvas stretched across the sky,
With dreams as colors that never die.

So let us wander, hand in hand,
Across the infinite, timeless land.
With every glance, a world reborn,
In polished gussets, futures worn.

Winter's

Snowflakes dance in the air,
Whispers soft as a prayer.
Blankets cover the ground,
In this peace, joy is found.

Frosty breath in the night,
Stars above shining bright.
A world wrapped in pure white,
Nature's hush, pure delight.

Footprints lead through the pine,
Each step marks a design.
Crystals glisten and gleam,
In this chill, we can dream.

Children laugh and they play,
Building castles today.
The warmth of hearts unite,
Underneath the moonlight.

As the sun starts to fade,
In this magic, we stayed.
Winter's song takes its flight,
Bringing calm to the night.

Cosmic Frost

Stars twinkle in the deep,
Galaxies swirl in their sleep.
Nebulas glow soft and bright,
Draping the cosmos in light.

Planets spin in a dance,
In the cosmos, we glance.
Frosty whispers ascend,
Time and space gently bend.

Meteor trails cut the sky,
As we watch them zoom by.
Frozen wonders appear,
In the vastness, we cheer.

Black holes concealed in the dark,
Infinite secrets they embark.
The universe, vast and grand,
Holds the beauty we understand.

Amidst the celestial plot,
We find solace in thought.
Cosmic frost, a surreal sight,
In the expanse of the night.

Silent Nightfall

The dusk envelops the trees,
Crisp air carries a breeze.
Shadows stretch across the lane,
Whispers echo, soft as rain.

Twilight paints the world low,
Softly wrapped in its glow.
Stars emerge, one by one,
In the silence, the day's done.

Crickets sing their night song,
In the dark, we belong.
Moonlight spills on the ground,
In this stillness, peace is found.

Rustling leaves in the wood,
Nature's pulse, understood.
The night cradles the light,
In its arms, we feel right.

As we breathe in the calm,
Hearts embrace the soothing balm.
Silent nightfall, so near,
Wraps us close, holds us dear.

Glimmering Tranquility

Morning dew on the grass,
Time seems slow as we pass.
Sunrise casts golden rays,
In this light, we laze.

Birds chirp a gentle tune,
Welcoming the day's soon.
Soft petals bloom with grace,
Nature smiles, finds its place.

Rivers flow, a soft sound,
Welcoming where dreams abound.
Clouds drift with blissful ease,
Spreading calm like the breeze.

As the hours unfold wide,
We find peace in the tide.
Glimmers of hope arise,
Underneath the vast skies.

In this dance of the day,
Let our worries drift away.
Tranquility's soft kiss,
Holds our hearts in pure bliss.

Flurries of Light

Soft whispers of twilight,
Dancing in the air,
Stars twinkle above,
Magic everywhere.

Gentle flakes descend,
Kissing the ground below,
A canvas of white forms,
In the moon's soft glow.

Echoes of laughter ring,
Children play and spin,
Creating snow angels,
Let the fun begin.

Night wraps around us,
In a warm embrace,
Time seems to stand still,
In this magical place.

Hope flutters like wings,
In the chilly night breeze,
Dreams drift like snowflakes,
Bringing hearts to ease.

Cooled by the Cosmos

The heavens stretch wide,
In hues of deep blue,
Stars shimmer softly,
Whispers of the new.

Galaxies spiral,
In romantic ballet,
The night sky invites,
Wonder's grand display.

Planets spin gently,
In their timeless dance,
Magic is alive,
In this cosmic expanse.

Comets blaze like fire,
Across the vast dome,
While stardust lingers,
A reminder of home.

Cool breezes surround,
As the night unfolds,
The universe breathes,
In stories untold.

Celestial Winter

Winter's embrace tightens,
With a cold, silvery ring,
The moon hangs so low,
As nightbirds sing.

Crystals in the air,
Reflect light's gentle grace,
Nature's frozen artwork,
In every space.

Trees wear white blankets,
So tranquil and still,
Underneath their cover,
Dreams quietly fill.

Frosty breaths linger,
In the cool, crisp air,
Each moment enchanted,
Beyond compare.

Within this stillness,
Magic finds its way,
Whispers of the stars,
Guide us till the day.

Glistening Dreams

In the quiet night,
A shimmer does unfold,
Dreams dance like starlight,
In tales to be told.

Every snowflake falls,
As if kissed by light,
Creating a tapestry,
Of pure delight.

The world is aglow,
With glimmers of hope,
Each moment cherished,
As we learn to cope.

Hearts gleam like diamonds,
In this soft embrace,
Finding warmth in dreams,
As we share this space.

So let lights guide us,
Through shadows and schemes,
For in the stillness,
We weave glistening dreams.

Distant Echoes of Dreams Unseen

Whispers dance on silent winds,
Carrying hopes that never end.
Fleeting shadows, soft and bright,
Reaching out through endless night.

In the stillness, secrets dwell,
Casting spells we cannot tell.
Voices call from far away,
Guiding hearts to light the day.

Through the vale of time we stride,
With our dreams as our true guide.
Stars above begin to gleam,
Sparking life within each dream.

Silent echoes call us near,
Bringing visions crystal clear.
In those dreams we'll find our way,
To the dawn of a new day.

A Star Beyond the Chill

In the night, a bright star glows,
Casting warmth as cold winds blow.
Guiding hearts with gentle light,
Bringing hope to darkest night.

Through the frost, it shines so clear,
Whispering tales for those who hear.
A beacon for the lost and lone,
It invites us to dream and roam.

Each twinkle tells a tale of grace,
Time suspended in a sacred space.
Endless paths spiral ever wide,
With that star as our faithful guide.

Though the chill may bite and sting,
In its glow, our spirits spring.
A reminder that through the dark,
A single spark ignites the heart.

Touch of Frost upon Dreams

Frosted whispers kiss the ground,
In the silence, magic found.
Dreams emerge like morning dew,
Glimmers of a world anew.

Softly painting all we see,
Nature's brush, a symphony.
Every flake, a fleeting chance,
In this cold, a sweet romance.

As the dawn begins to break,
Frosty realms start to awake.
With each sparkle, hope takes flight,
Carried on the morning light.

Touch of frost, a gentle hand,
On the dreams where we will stand.
In the quiet of the morn,
New adventures will be born.

Musing Under a Silvery Veil

Beneath the moon's soft silver glow,
Whispers of the night bestow.
Thoughts that drift like autumn leaves,
In a world where magic weaves.

Stars like jewels in the sky,
Glimmer as the night winds sigh.
Each moment wrapped in mystery,
Inviting us to simply be.

Underneath this silken light,
Dreams emerge from shadows bright.
Moments shared, a precious gift,
As hearts and spirits gently lift.

Softly wrapped in night's embrace,
Finding solace in this space.
Musing on what lies ahead,
Underneath the stars we tread.

Moonbeams on the Frozen Path

Moonlight dances on the frost,
Whispers secrets, never lost.
Silvery beams on ice they spread,
Softly guiding where we tread.

Shadows stretch beneath the trees,
Carried softly by the breeze.
A tranquil path of shimmering light,
Invites the wanderer's delight.

Footsteps crunching, crisp and clear,
Nature's echo, calm and near.
Each breath a mist upon the air,
Magic lingers everywhere.

Glistening crystals, cold yet bright,
Reflect the beauty of the night.
In this realm of frozen dreams,
The world is lost in lunar gleams.

So let your heart be free to roam,
In the moon's embrace, find your home.
The frozen path will warmly glow,
With secrets that the night may show.

Calming Lullabies from the Cosmos

In the silence of the night,
Stars sing softly, pure delight.
Cosmic whispers float on high,
Carried gently through the sky.

Celestial lullabies unfold,
Stories of the brave and bold.
Each twinkling star a note that plays,
Guiding dreams through starry ways.

Moonlit serenades embrace,
Cradled in the universe's grace.
A symphony of worlds afar,
Sings of peace beneath the stars.

Close your eyes and feel the flow,
Of tranquil waves that come and go.
In this vast celestial sea,
Rest your soul, and simply be.

With each breath, let worries fade,
As cosmic melodies invade.
The universe holds tight its song,
A comforting embrace, all night long.

Starry Enchantment

Under the blanket of the night,
Stars awaken, feeling bright.
Winking softly, casting lore,
Enchanting dreams forevermore.

Galaxies swirl in endless rows,
Whispers of light, secrets they close.
Captured hearts in wonder strung,
As the universe softly hums.

Magic lingers in the dark,
Each constellation, a lover's spark.
Chasing shadows, weaving fate,
In the twilight, we contemplate.

Timeless tales in the sky reside,
Leaving traces, like a guide.
With every blink, a new desire,
Light ignites the heart's own fire.

Boundless beauty, vast and free,
Casts our spirits to be.
In this starry realm we find,
An enchanting peace for the mind.

The Frosty Artistry of Night

Frosted trees in silver dress,
Nature painted, pure finesse.
Intricate patterns weave and flow,
A masterpiece in moonlit glow.

Crystalline droplets catch the light,
Twinkling softly, pure delight.
Each branch adorned with icy lace,
Nature's art, a timeless grace.

In the stillness, magic reigns,
Whispers drift on frosty panes.
A tranquil world dressed in white,
Holds the secrets of the night.

As shadows stretch and softly creep,
The frosty silence lulls to sleep.
Every breath, a cloud of dreams,
In this night, reality seems.

Let the artistry unfold,
In every flake, a story told.
Embrace the beauty, take it in,
Where night and frost together spin.

Frosty Horizon

The morning glows with a chill,
Snowflakes dance on the wind,
A canvas of white unbroken,
Whispers of winter begin.

Icicles hang from the eaves,
Nature's glittering designs,
Each breath forms a misty cloud,
As daylight softly shines.

Frozen lakes hold secrets deep,
Reflecting the clear blue sky,
Footprints trace a quiet path,
As the world breathes a sigh.

Trees adorned in icy coats,
Branches bow with the weight,
Every twig a crystal shard,
In this frosty landscape.

The horizon calls us to roam,
A wonderland waiting near,
In the stillness we find peace,
Where the heart sheds its fear.

Ethereal Nightfall

As twilight cloaks the day,
Stars awaken one by one,
The moon hangs like a pearl,
In the canvas of night done.

Shadows stretch across the land,
With secrets held in their folds,
Whispers float on the cool breeze,
As the evening softly unfolds.

The sky turns a violet hue,
A tapestry woven with dreams,
Crickets sing their lullabies,
To rivers flowing in streams.

In this realm of shimmering light,
Mysteries dance on the edge,
Every heartbeat a soft echo,
In the night's gentle pledge.

Time slows to a gentle pause,
Wrapped in the night's embrace,
Here, in the ethereal glow,
We find our sacred space.

Whispered Secrets of the Cosmos

Beneath the vast celestial dome,
Stars twinkle with forgotten lore,
Galaxies spin in silent dance,
Revealing what the heart longs for.

Comets streak through endless night,
Charting paths through darkest skies,
Each spark a story from the past,
Eliciting wonder and sighs.

Moonlight kisses the earth so sweet,
Soft as a lover's gentle breath,
Illuminating paths unknown,
In shadows whispering of death.

Constellations tell a tale,
Of heroes, lovers, and fates,
In the stillness, we listen close,
To the universe that waits.

Time flows like a gentle stream,
Eternity's whispers surround,
In the cosmos, secrets linger,
In the silence, we're unbound.

Icy Celestial Ballet

In the sky, the stars align,
Dancing in a cosmic show,
With ribbons of light unfurling,
A celestial ballet aglow.

Frozen landscapes reflect dreams,
As comets pirouette and glide,
Each movement a graceful whisper,
In the universe's wide tide.

Nebulas swirl in colors bright,
Like paint on a cosmic brush,
Creating a canvas alive,
Where galaxies come and hush.

The night hums with endless rhythms,
Echoing through the infinite sea,
In the ballet of time and space,
All are part of this harmony.

As we gaze upon the heavens,
Hearts beat in synchronicity,
In the icy celestial dance,
We find our place in eternity.

Stars on Ice

In the midnight sky so clear,
Stars reflect like diamonds near.
Frozen lakes where dreams reside,
Whispers of the cosmos glide.

Glimmers dance upon the frost,
In their light, no love is lost.
Cold embraces, gentle sighs,
Life beneath the frozen skies.

Silent echoes, crystal bright,
Veils of beauty, pure delight.
Underneath the icy sheen,
Wonders in the night unseen.

Shimmering in the stillness deep,
Secrets that the cosmos keep.
Stars on ice, a timeless tale,
A celestial, frozen trail.

Chilling Luminescence

A glow that warms the frigid air,
Chilling luminescence rare.
In shadows soft, the colors flow,
A dance of light beneath the snow.

Frosty crystals gleam and shine,
Nature's canvas, pure design.
In the dark, there's life anew,
Painting dreams in shades of blue.

Each flicker tells a story sweet,
Of worlds beyond where spirits meet.
In the dusk, their whispers rise,
Echoes of forgotten skies.

Cool embrace of evening's grace,
Stars illuminate this place.
Chilling luminescence, bright,
Guiding hearts through winter's night.

Frigid Moonlight

In frigid rays the moonlight gleams,
Casting silver on my dreams.
A gentle kiss of icy air,
Whispers float, serene and rare.

Beneath the glow, the shadows creep,
Secrets that the night must keep.
Frozen echoes breathe and sigh,
Telling tales of those who fly.

Moonlit paths of glistening white,
Guide the wanderers of the night.
Each step writes a story new,
In the frost, the heart is true.

Frigid moonlight, calm and bright,
Wraps the world in soft twilight.
A silver touch upon the ground,
In stillness, peace can be found.

Whispering Nebulae

In darkened depths where starlight fades,
Whispering nebulae, soft cascades.
Colors swirl in cosmic grace,
Dreams unfold in endless space.

Veils of mystery, soft and light,
Guide the souls who yearn for flight.
Galaxies drift, a dance unfolds,
A tapestry of stories told.

In the hush of infinite night,
Stars ignite with pure delight.
Cosmic secrets softly share,
In the depths, true wonders stare.

Nebulae weave a gentle song,
In their arms, we all belong.
Whispering through the velvet sky,
A universal lullaby.

Beneath a Shimmering Canopy

In the woods where shadows dance,
Stars above weave dreams by chance.
Leaves whisper secrets to the night,
Moonlight filters, soft and bright.

Branches stretch like gentle hands,
Guarding magic in these lands.
Crickets sing a lullaby,
Nature's tune, a sweet goodbye.

The air is filled with fragrant pine,
An embrace, both warm and fine.
Beneath this sky of endless blue,
Nature's heart beats strong and true.

Night unfolds with silver grace,
In this tranquil, sacred space.
Every breeze a tender sigh,
Beneath stars that never die.

Frosty Whispers of the Universe

In the stillness, cold and clear,
Frozen whispers brush the ear.
Stars above, like diamonds gleam,
Crackling ice, a crystal dream.

The cosmos hums a distant song,
Where the frosty tales belong.
Galaxies in silent flight,
A ballet in the heart of night.

Beneath the veil of winter's breath,
Lies a beauty born of death.
Each flake falls with grace divine,
Whispers echo, intertwine.

Cold embraces time and space,
In its arms, we find our place.
Universes spin and sway,
Frosty whispers lead the way.

Frozen Echoes of Night's Heart

Beneath the moon's watchful eye,
Whispers linger, soft and shy.
Echoes dance in frosty air,
Night reveals its hidden flair.

Each shadow tells a tale untold,
Of brave nights, of memories bold.
Stars align, a silver chart,
Mapping out the night's warm heart.

Silence wraps the earth in peace,
As frozen dreams begin to cease.
A gentle touch, a soft caress,
In this realm, we feel our stress.

Ice-kissed whispers fill the space,
With every breath, a soft embrace.
Frozen echoes, sweet and rare,
In the stillness, we lay bare.

Echoing Fantasies on a Crisp Night

Underneath the starlit skies,
Dreams take flight, the spirit cries.
Crisp air carries tales anew,
Night unfolds its velvet hue.

Whispers float on gentle sighs,
Echoing beneath cosmic lies.
Moonbeams scatter, dance and play,
Guiding lost souls on their way.

Fantasy blooms in shadows deep,
While the world around us sleeps.
Crickets chirp a rhythmic tune,
Beneath the watchful eye of moon.

With each heartbeat, dreams revive,
In this moment, we're alive.
Echoing fantasies take flight,
On the canvas of the night.

Shadows Caressed by Light

In the gentle glow of day,
Shadows dance and play,
A soft whisper flows,
Nature wakes and grows.

Between the branches high,
The sun begins to sigh,
As colors start to blend,
And dreams find their end.

Golden rays, they leap,
In quiet, secrets keep,
Dancing on the ground,
Harmony is found.

Softly evening calls,
As daylight gently falls,
With a touch so light,
Shadows kiss the night.

In the twilight's hue,
The world feels anew,
In this tender sight,
Shadows caressed by light.

Luminous Nightfall

A canvas draped in blue,
Stars begin to strew,
Whispers fill the air,
As magic finds its lair.

Moonlight spills like wine,
A radiant design,
With a silver glow,
The darkness starts to flow.

Beneath the watchful skies,
With dreams that softly rise,
Each twinkle, a delight,
In the luminous night.

Crickets serenade the gloom,
Filling hearts with bloom,
While shadows linger near,
Embraced by night so clear.

With every passing hour,
The night displays its power,
As slumber drapes the land,
Luminous nightfall's hand.

Night's Embrace on Chilly Breaths

In the chill of night's air,
Breaths of fog appear,
Hushed whispers unfold,
As the stars behold.

The moon hangs low and bright,
Casting dreams in light,
While leaves in shadows sway,
As the night steals the day.

A blanket cool and deep,
Inviting souls to sleep,
Wrapped in nature's sigh,
Under the sprawling sky.

Every rustle and sound,
In silence is found,
Chilly breaths embrace,
This serene, quiet space.

With night as a friend,
Adventures never end,
In this tranquil dance,
Night's embrace, a chance.

Whims of the Cool Twilight

As daylight bids goodbye,
The colors sigh and vie,
With hints of purple hues,
And whispers of the blues.

Twilight teases the eye,
In playful, soft reply,
With secrets it will share,
In the gentle evening air.

Breezes weave through the trees,
With every rustling breeze,
As fireflies take flight,
In whims of the night.

The world slows down its pace,
In this magical space,
Where dreams begin to thread,
In twilight's calming bed.

With the sky turning dark,
Leaving behind a spark,
Whims of the cool twilight,
Bring comfort, pure delight.

Nocturnal Embrace

In the stillness of the night,
Stars whisper secrets bright,
Moonlight drapes the sleeping earth,
A tapestry of silent mirth.

Gentle winds caress the trees,
Carrying a soothing breeze,
Shadows dance upon the ground,
In this peace, we are found.

Night wraps us in its cloak,
Each heartbeat, a tender stroke,
Dreams take flight on silver wings,
In our hearts, the night still sings.

Underneath the celestial dome,
Every star a distant home,
We find solace, hand in hand,
In this vast and quiet land.

Beneath the gaze of the moon's eye,
Whispers of the darkened sky,
In nocturnal embrace we dwell,
Within the night's enchanting spell.

Night's Frosted Breath

Chill of evening, crisp and clear,
Breath of night, distinct and near,
Frosty patterns touch the glass,
As if time begins to pass.

Whispers linger in the air,
Carried softly, a timeless prayer,
Underneath the winter's gaze,
Stars ignited in frosty haze.

Trees adorned with shimmering frost,
Nature's beauty, never lost,
Each branch a story, softly told,
Of nights where dreams unfold.

As shadows stretch and darkness grows,
Silent paths, where moonlight flows,
Every breath a fleeting sigh,
In the night, we learn to fly.

Cloaked in stillness, hearts entwined,
Amidst the night, a truth we find,
In the frost, life holds its worth,
Breathing beauty into the earth.

Ethereal Glow

In twilight's soft, enchanting light,
Dreams begin to take their flight,
A world awash in gentle hues,
Painting skies in vibrant blues.

Whispers linger in the dawn,
Moments cherished, never gone,
With every pulse, a story shared,
In the glow, we are bared.

Stars awaken in the shroud,
Glowing softly, daring, proud,
They guide us through the endless night,
Showing paths with gentle light.

Each flicker is a hopeful sign,
A reminder of the divine,
In the ethereal, we are free,
Boundless as the deep blue sea.

Wrapped in magic, hearts ignite,
In harmony, we take flight,
Under the glow of cosmic streams,
We are one, lost in dreams.

Glistening Shadows

As twilight paints the world in gray,
Shadows dance, then fade away,
Glistening under whispers low,
The hidden tales we long to know.

In corners where the light retreats,
Mysteries and silence meet,
Each shadow holds a whispered thought,
Secrets of the night they've sought.

Glistening hearts in twilight's embrace,
Every glance, a lingering trace,
In the dark, our spirits soar,
Finding hope on unseen shores.

The world is hushed, the night is near,
In each moment, we hold dear,
Shadows glisten with tales untold,
In this magic, we behold.

With every step, the night unfolds,
A tapestry of dreams retold,
In glistening shadows, we transcend,
In the dark, our souls will mend.

Dreams Wrapped in Moonlight

In the hush of a quiet night,
Whispers dance in silver light.
Stars above blink in delight,
As dreams take flight till morning bright.

Gentle breezes softly sigh,
Carrying wishes way up high.
While shadows weave a lullaby,
Underneath the starlit sky.

Mysterious paths begin to form,
Guided by a mysterious norm.
In the realm where dreams will swarm,
Hearts find peace, a tranquil warm.

Mystic glows enshroud the earth,
Echoes of laughter, joy, and mirth.
In the moonlight, dreams find birth,
A promise of infinite worth.

Awake or asleep, we intertwine,
In the moon's glow, our souls combine.
Wrapped in dreams, our spirits shine,
In the night, love's pure design.

Frozen Twilight's Embrace

In the stillness of dusk's first chill,
A blanket of frost begins to fill.
Whispers of winter, soft yet shrill,
Time fleeting, yet life stands still.

Branches glisten, twinkling bright,
Cascading snow in fading light.
The world, a canvas, pure and white,
Painted in hues of quiet delight.

Silence lingers, a soft caress,
Shrouded in nature's cold finesse.
Within this peace, we find our rest,
As twilight wraps us, gently blessed.

Memories gather, softly spun,
Under the gaze of the setting sun.
Hearts beat slowly, one by one,
In frozen twilight, dreams begun.

As shadows blend in winter's fold,
Tales of warmth and love unfold.
In frozen moments, memories hold,
A timeless story quietly told.

Luminous Shadows

Beneath the glow of softest night,
Shadows dance, embracing light.
In the stillness, dreams take flight,
Echoing whispers, a sweet delight.

Moonbeams weave through branches bare,
Illuminating secrets we share.
Luminous glow in the evening air,
Filling hearts with tender care.

The world glimmers, crisp and bright,
Figures move in soft twilight.
Hidden wishes, pure and slight,
Shadows play with thoughts of light.

Every corner softly brightens,
As the tapestry of dreams heightens.
In the darkness, hope ignites,
Luminous shadows banish frights.

In the dance of night we seek,
Mirrors of love, both strong and weak.
Together we find solace, speak,
In luminous shadows, futures unique.

Afterglow of a Winter's Dream

As dawn breaks on the frosted morn,
Silent whispers of night are born.
In the air, pure magic, worn,
From dreams that glow, and hearts adorned.

Tendrils of light stretch across the land,
Painting silver streams, oh so grand.
Nature holds us in her hand,
In afterglow, we make our stand.

Snowflakes shimmer in warming rays,
Guiding us through the winter maze.
In the afterglow, our spirits blaze,
Awakening joy, as the heart sways.

Moments catch in the vibrant hues,
Echoes of laughter, hopes, and views.
In the stillness, love renews,
Carried by winds, a gentle muse.

With each step through this dream-like scene,
Memories linger, soft and serene.
In the afterglow, magic is keen,
A winter's embrace, forever green.

Starlight in Hibernation

Stars asleep in velvet skies,
Dreams of light in quiet sighs.
Whispers of the darkened years,
Crystals form from silent tears.

Winter's breath on frozen ground,
Mysteries in silence found.
Hibernating, all's at peace,
While the world begins to cease.

Beneath the frost, new blooms await,
Nature's pause, an ancient fate.
Starlight waits with bated breath,
In the stillness, life and death.

Hope will rise with morning's glow,
Through the ice, the green will show.
Dreamers' hearts, they beat in time,
To the rhythm, soft and prime.

So let the stars, in slumber deep,
Guard the secrets that they keep.
In their light, we find our way,
Through the night and into day.

Midnight's Frozen Canvas

Midnight casts its chilling spell,
On frozen streets where echoes dwell.
Painted moons in silver hue,
Art of night, a world anew.

Stars like diamonds, crisp and bright,
Dancing softly, pure delight.
Whispers swathe the wintry air,
Cradling dreams without a care.

Every shadow tells a tale,
Of timeless journeys, soft and frail.
The world, a canvas broad and wide,
Where every heart can safely hide.

Frozen branches reach for dreams,
Woven in the night's soft seams.
With every breath, the silence sings,
Of fleeting nights and gentle wings.

When dawn breaks, the tales shall fade,
Yet in our hearts, the art is made.
Hold the night, as shadows grow,
In frozen strokes, our spirits flow.

Gleaming Veils of the Night

Veils of night, a soft embrace,
Whispers of a secret place.
Crimson skies begin to part,
Hiding dreams within the heart.

Gleaming stars with silent grace,
Brush the dark, a fleeting trace.
Every twinkle, stories told,
Of brave hearts, both young and old.

Moonlight dances on the ground,
In its glow, hope is found.
In the shadows, fears take flight,
As shadows meld with dreams of light.

Wrapped in coats of silken dark,
We wander forth to leave a mark.
With every whisper, magic grows,
In the night, the heart bestows.

Through the haze where silence sighs,
Endless wonders fill the skies.
Embrace the night, let spirits soar,
In gleaming veils forevermore.

Whispered Frost

Frosty breath upon the air,
Whispers echo everywhere.
Nature's shiver, soft and light,
Bringing tales from deep of night.

Trees adorned with sparkling lace,
Glistening in their frozen grace.
Each crystal forms a silent song,
In the night where dreams belong.

Footsteps echo on the ground,
In the stillness, peace is found.
Every shadow holds a truth,
From the heart of ancient youth.

As the stars begin to fade,
Morning whispers, unafraid.
Through the frost, the new day gleams,
A tapestry of waking dreams.

So let the night wrap us tight,
In whispered frost, we find our light.
In every breath, a promise flows,
As the warmth of daylight grows.

Quietude Beneath the Firmament

Beneath the stars, a hush prevails,
As moonlight bathes the silver trails,
A tranquil night, the world at peace,
In quietude, all troubles cease.

The whispers of the gentle breeze,
Embrace the trees, the rustling leaves,
Soft shadows dance in moon's soft glow,
Where dreams are born, and worries flow.

Each twinkling light, a story told,
Of ancient times, of hearts so bold,
The sky, a canvas vast and wide,
In stillness, secrets choose to hide.

The night unfolds its velvet arms,
Protecting all from earthly harms,
In peaceful slumber, spirits soar,
Beneath the firmament, they explore.

So pause awhile, let silence reign,
In quietude, we shed the strain,
Embracing night, our souls take flight,
In harmony, we greet the night.

Snowflakes under Celestial Gaze

Snowflakes drift on whispered sighs,
Underneath the vast, clear skies,
They twirl and dance in moon's embrace,
Creating magic, a soft lace.

Each flake a wonder, unique in flight,
Glistening gems in the pale light,
They blanket earth with a serene quilt,
A wondrous beauty, softly built.

Under celestial gaze so bright,
They shimmer softly through the night,
A tapestry of white and blue,
As starlight kisses every hue.

In silent air, they find their rest,
A fleeting moment, nature's best,
They whisper tales of winter's grace,
In quietude, they find their place.

So let us marvel, hearts alive,
As snowflakes drift and gently thrive,
Underneath the sky's embrace,
In winter's dance, we find our space.

Winter's Veil Over Dreamland

A gentle hush descends at night,
Winter's veil, a blanket white,
In dreams, the world is softly wrapped,
In cozy warmth, our hopes are tapped.

Silent whispers fill the air,
Dreamland calls with tender care,
Each flicker of a candle's flame,
A cherished moment, softly named.

The moonlight weaves through frosted trees,
In tranquil nights, the heart finds ease,
The stars like pearls against the dark,
Illuminate each hopeful spark.

As shadows linger, time stands still,
In winter's magic, hearts we fill,
With visions sweet and memories bright,
In dreamland's glow, we find our light.

So let us wander through the night,
Wrapped in dreams, our spirits bright,
With winter's veil, we softly tread,
In tranquil peace, our souls are led.

A Canvas of Stars Unfurled

In the night, a canvas wide,
Stars like diamonds, side by side,
Each twinkling light, a wish in flight,
Painting dreams in the velvet night.

They whisper secrets from afar,
Guiding ships, a cosmic star,
With every glance, a story spun,
A universe where all is one.

Galaxies dance in cosmic grace,
In quiet awe, we find our place,
Amongst the wonders, brave and bold,
In starlit tales, our hearts unfold.

The night draws close, yet feels so near,
A symphony that we can hear,
In every spark, a heartbeat flows,
As peace and harmony bestows.

So lift your gaze and breathe it in,
The wonders of the night begin,
With every star, a new dream swirled,
A canvas bright in cosmos unfurled.

A Winter's Lullaby

Softly falls the snow tonight,
Blanketing the world in white.
Gentle whispers, cold and bright,
Nature's song, serene delight.

Stars above like diamonds gleam,
In the silence, dreams redeem.
Crystals dance, a frosty theme,
Winter's hush, a waking dream.

Frosted branches, glittering fine,
As the moon begins to shine.
Lullabies of snow entwine,
Hearing peace in every line.

Crisp and clean, the midnight air,
Wrapped in warmth, without a care.
Close your eyes, let dreams repair,
In this wintry world so rare.

Through the night, the cold winds sigh,
Singing low a soft goodbye.
Hold this moment, sweetly nigh,
Beneath the frosty velvet sky.

Under the Veil of Night

Under the veil of night so deep,
Stars awake while children sleep.
Moonlight casts its silver glow,
Painting shadows down below.

Whispers drift upon the breeze,
Stirring softly through the trees.
Every branch, a secret keeps,
In this world where magic peeps.

Dreamers roam the darkened lanes,
Chasing hopes like falling rains.
Echoed laughter, fleeting dreams,
In the night, nothing's as it seems.

In the hush, the heart can hear,
Voices rising, crystal clear.
Mysteries dance upon the air,
Shadows sigh, without a care.

Draped in velvet skies above,
Stars connect like threads of love.
Each heartbeat finds its place tonight,
Bound together, soft and light.

Icy Murmurs in the Dark

Icy murmurs fill the night,
Whispers cool, a ghostly flight.
Frozen breezes brush my face,
In the dark, I find my place.

Crystalline echoes swirl around,
Gentle sighs without a sound.
Every stroke, a touch of frost,
In the quiet, dreams embossed.

Glistening trails of moonlit streams,
Nighttime weaves its silver dreams.
Beneath the stars, the world feels small,
In this stillness, I hear it call.

Frosted whispers, secrets wane,
Each breath mingles with the rain.
Shadows dance on icy floors,
Memories stir, behind closed doors.

In the dark, the chill brings peace,
Offering solace, sweet release.
Holding tight, I feel the spark,
Of icy murmurs in the dark.

Celestial Whispers in the Wind

Celestial whispers in the wind,
Stories from where dreams begin.
Gentle sighs of distant stars,
Bringing light from afar.

Windswept tales, soft and low,
Breathe a melody we know.
Time stands still, the world awakes,
In the hush, the silence breaks.

Each breeze carries ancient lore,
Secrets shared from shore to shore.
Floating hopes in twilight's reach,
Nature speaks, if we would listen, teach.

Chasing shadows, lost in dreams,
With every gust, the moment gleams.
Follow paths where silence roams,
In whispers, this world feels like home.

Through the night, let spirits lead,
In celestial whispers, take heed.
Feel the magic, let it bloom,
Guide your heart through every room.

Serenade of Celestial Whispers

Underneath the velvet sky,
Stars flicker in a soft sigh,
Moonlight weaves a silver song,
Carried where the dreams belong.

Night unfolds her gentle grace,
In this vast, enchanted space,
Echoes dance on breezes light,
Painting shadows with pure delight.

Whispers float on cosmic streams,
Binding hope within our dreams,
Every twinkle tells a tale,
As the universe exhales.

Waves of silence rise and fall,
Eternity begins to call,
In the hush, we find our peace,
In this moment, all increase.

So let each star guide your way,
In the night, forever stay,
With sweet whispers from above,
Wrapped in ever-living love.

Cosmic Chill

A breeze whispers through the night,
Carrying dreams in soft flight,
Cold stars twinkle from afar,
Each one a guiding, distant star.

Silence wraps the world in peace,
Underneath this cosmic fleece,
Time seems to hold its breath tight,
In the heart of endless night.

Frozen air bites tender skin,
Yet warmth blooms from deep within,
Thoughts drift like the snowflakes fall,
In the quiet, love's the call.

Stillness reigns, the heartbeats slow,
In the dark, we learn to grow,
Finding solace in the chill,
Underneath the moon's bright will.

With each breath, the cosmos sighs,
As galaxies spin in the skies,
In this moment, pure and free,
We embrace eternity.

A Constellation of Quiet Moments

In stillness, time takes flight,
Moments twinkle, soft and bright,
Thoughts emerge like stars in bloom,
Lighting up the vastest room.

Each breath whispers a new song,
In this world where we belong,
Silent echoes fill the air,
A symphony stripped bare.

The universe in quiet flow,
Hints of magic in the glow,
Suspended in the space between,
Where the unseen is felt keen.

Every heartbeat tells a truth,
Woven through the threads of youth,
Moments linger, softly spun,
Like the dance of moon and sun.

In these constellations found,
Each whisper adds to the sound,
Let us savor every sigh,
In the stillness, you and I.

Night's Whispering Edge

At the edge where shadows play,
Night unfolds her rich array,
Softly singing to the stars,
Guiding dreams from near to far.

Every rustle lifts the veil,
In the dark, we find our trail,
Silence speaks in echoes clear,
Carried gently, sweet and near.

Veils of twilight softly dance,
Inviting hearts to take a chance,
In the chill, the warmth ignites,
Giving life to starry nights.

Time stands still on night's long edge,
In this moment, make a pledge,
Listen closely, feel the peace,
In the dark, all worries cease.

So breathe in the midnight air,
Let it lighten every care,
On night's whispering edge we stand,
Together, hand in hand.

Whispers of the Midnight Breeze

In the hush of night's embrace,
The whispers dance with grace.
Stars above softly gleam,
In this tranquil, moonlit dream.

A gentle rustle in the trees,
Carried on the playful breeze.
Secrets spoken, soft and low,
Only the night sky can know.

Shadows waltz upon the ground,
As the world slows to a sound.
Silver light begins to play,
Chasing all our cares away.

Listen close to night's refrain,
A song that eases every pain.
In this moment, all is still,
Heart and soul begin to fill.

With every gust, a promise made,
In these hours, fears will fade.
Whispers on the winds of night,
Bring us calm, bring us light.

Celestial Frost

In the stillness of the night,
Frost glimmers, pure and white.
Crystals formed on pane and tree,
Nature's art for all to see.

Moonlight kisses every flake,
Silent beauty, soft as ache.
Winter whispers in the dark,
A frosty glow, a subtle spark.

Footsteps crunch on icy ground,
In this peace, solace found.
Stars like diamonds in the sky,
Underneath this night, we sigh.

Breath like clouds that dance and swirl,
In the chill, magic unfurls.
Frosted dreams begin to weave,
In this world, we dare believe.

With each sigh, the air turns cold,
But within, warmth to behold.
Celestial frost, a tender gift,
Guiding hearts through winter's drift.

Nocturnal Serenade

Underneath the velvet skies,
Night unfolds with quiet sighs.
Crickets sing in soft refrain,
Melodies of sweet, sweet pain.

The moon, a lantern, softly glows,
While gentle shadows start to doze.
Stars drift by, a fleeting tune,
Whispers of the evening moon.

Dreamers wander, hearts aglow,
In the night's enchanting flow.
Time stands still, each breath a song,
In this magic, we belong.

Swaying trees join in the play,
As the night enchants the day.
In this silent, sweet cascade,
Lies the beauty of a serenade.

Harmony within the dark,
Echoes of a distant lark.
Nocturnal dreams drift and sail,
In this calm, we shall prevail.

Echoes of the Winter Sky

Beneath the vast and frosty dome,
Winter whispers, calling home.
Echoes dance in chilled twilight,
As the stars emerge, so bright.

The air, crisp with tales untold,
Magic drapes like threads of gold.
Silhouettes against the white,
Nature weaves its soft delight.

Muffled sounds of distant cheer,
Wrap around like warmth, so near.
Each breath comes with a ghostly trace,
In this frozen, sacred space.

Winds carry laughter through the trees,
In this moment, hearts feel ease.
Whispers of the past, they flow,
Painting memories in the snow.

In this silence, dreams arise,
Underneath the winter skies.
Echoes of a world so bright,
Cradle us in winter's light.

Chilling Serenades of the Cosmos

Whispers of stars call me near,
Echoes of dreams, soft and clear.
Darkness wraps in velvet shroud,
Singing sweetly, quiet and loud.

Galaxies twinkle, the night aglow,
Wandering thoughts in the celestial flow.
Time drifts slowly on silky beams,
Lost in the magic of cosmic dreams.

Planets spin in their timeless waltz,
Aligning softly, with no faults.
Each breath I take, a note of grace,
Chilling serenades in this vast space.

Comets streak through the ink-black sky,
Painting tales as they flash by.
With every glance, I'm swept away,
In the arms of night, where shadows play.

A lullaby sung to the universe,
Soft tapping rhythms, silently terse.
Chilling serenades, a cosmic quest,
In starlit depths, my spirit rests.

Frosted Wishes on a Dark Night

Moonlight drapes the world in white,
Painting dreams on a winter night.
Footprints crunch on glistening snow,
Whispers of wishes begin to flow.

Stars above in a ballet,
Hold my secrets, keep them at bay.
Shadows dance under frosted trees,
Carried softly by the cold breeze.

A chill in the air, an enchanting thrill,
As heartbeats echo, time stands still.
Wishes float on the breath of air,
In the silent night, free from care.

Each flake tells a story of light,
In the hush of the deepening night.
Frosted wishes take their flight,
In the embrace of winter's white.

Underneath this endless sky,
Hope and wonder never shy.
Frosted wishes softly ignite,
Guiding my heart through the dark night.

Starlight's Embrace in the Stillness

Night unfolds with a gentle sigh,
Starlight glimmers, time drifts by.
In the stillness, magic breathes,
Wrapping dreams in softest sheaths.

The world below, a tranquil sight,
Bathed in whispers of silver light.
Crickets sing their lullabies,
As moonbeams dance in sleepy skies.

A canvas vast, of dreams untold,
Where every moment is pure gold.
In starlight's arms, worries release,
Here in the quiet, I find peace.

Constellations weave their tales,
From ancient times, through cosmic gales.
Embraced by light, my heart takes flight,
In the still of the gentle night.

Wrapped in a realm where dreams reside,
Beneath the stars, I'll always glide.
Starlight's embrace, forever mine,
In the stillness, our souls align.

Glimmers on a Silent Pond

Underneath a twilight sky,
Ripples stir, as shadows lie.
Whispers mingle with the breeze,
Nature's pulse flows with such ease.

Glimmers dance on water's face,
Painting scenes of quiet grace.
Each spark a promise, softly spun,
In stillness found, 'neath the setting sun.

The moon peeks in, a silver eye,
Reflecting dreams as they pass by.
Silent whispers brush the shore,
Calling forth the heart to soar.

An evening steeped in gentle sighs,
Where time slips by in soft goodbyes.
Glimmers wink in a tranquil breeze,
Enchanting moments, life's sweet tease.

With every breath, deep reflections grow,
In the pond's embrace, I find my flow.
Glimmers shine, time gently nods,
In silence shared, I meet the gods.

Subtle Nightscape

Underneath the velvet sky,
Stars whisper soft and low,
A gentle breeze holds secrets,
As shadows dance and flow.

Moonlight bathes the quiet earth,
Painting dreams in silver hues,
While nightingale's sweet song rises,
Carrying the night's soft muse.

Crickets serenade the dark,
With rhythms pure and bright,
Every rustle tells a tale,
In the embrace of night.

Clouds drift like fleeting thoughts,
In a world of calm and peace,
Mysteries unfold in layers,
As the heart finds its release.

The stars blink in secret code,
A language of the sky,
In this subtle nightscape,
Awakens dreams that fly.

Shivering Cosmos

Lost in the vastness above,
Galaxies spin and twirl,
Each distant star a heartbeat,
In the shivering swirl.

Nebulae glow, a phantom light,
Whispers of ancient time,
A cosmic dance we can't perceive,
In rhythm and in rhyme.

Eons pass like fleeting thoughts,
In the fabric of the night,
Where wonders flutter softly,
In a boundless flight.

Planets cradle dreams unsaid,
As comets streak their trails,
A tapestry of fates entwined,
In the endless sails.

This universe, a fragile breath,
Petals on a breeze,
In the shivering cosmos,
Our souls find their ease.

Freeze-frame Fantasies

Captured in a moment's grace,
Time stands still in light,
Memories dance like shadows,
In the cloak of twilight.

A child's laughter lingers sweet,
Echoes in golden air,
Every blink a lifetime,
In the stillness laid bare.

Framed in dreams, the colors blend,
Brushstrokes of the mind,
Each fantasy, a vivid scene,
In a world undefined.

Faces fade yet feelings stay,
In the heart's embrace,
Every freeze-frame, a story,
A moment we chase.

In this vast album of life,
We sift through time with ease,
Finding beauty in the brief,
In freeze-frame fantasies.

Night's Crystal Embrace

Wrapped in night's tender arms,
A hush descends so deep,
Stars twinkle like scattered gems,
As the world drifts to sleep.

Moonbeams weave through branches high,
Silhouettes softly weep,
While whispers float on velvet air,
In secrets that they keep.

Dreams take flight on silver wings,
Embraced by cosmic grace,
Every heartbeat finds its rhythm,
In the night's crystal embrace.

Gentle waves of softest night,
Cradle the weary mind,
In this sanctuary of peace,
A refuge we can find.

While starlight sketches stories,
Across the silent space,
We linger in the calmness,
Of night's crystal embrace.

Frost-kissed Dreams

In the still of night, a whisper flows,
Crystals gleam where the soft wind blows,
Blankets of white like a tender embrace,
In the frost-kissed dreams, we find our place.

Stars twinkle bright in the velvet sky,
Painting our hopes as we wander by,
Each breath a mist, with a chill so sweet,
We dance on the edge where worlds meet.

Moonlight glimmers on the frozen ground,
Every step taken, a magic found,
In the silence, the heart learns to sing,
Frost-kissed dreams, what joy they bring.

Nature hibernates, but our spirits soar,
With every heartbeat, we crave for more,
In winter's grip, we find our glow,
As dreams take flight, and the cold winds blow.

Hidden beneath, the green life waits,
Waiting for spring to open the gates,
Yet in this frost, our hearts will bloom,
In frost-kissed dreams, we find our room.

Secrets Spun from Stardust

In the quiet night, secrets unfold,
Whispers of stardust, tales untold,
Celestial wonders dance above,
Cradled in the arms of cosmic love.

Galaxies spin in a graceful sway,
Dreams woven in light, guiding our way,
Each twinkle a promise, hope intertwined,
In the web of the universe, we are aligned.

Nebulas cradle our wishes bright,
Painting the canvas of endless night,
With every breath, we share the grace,
Secrets spun from stardust, time and space.

Hearts are maps to the stars above,
Tracing the lines of our ancient love,
In every heartbeat, we sense the call,
Embracing the magic that binds us all.

In the vastness, we find our home,
Traveling the constellations, we freely roam,
For in every secret, and every song,
The fabric of stardust where we belong.

Twilight's Gentle Breath

As the sun dips low, colors ignite,
In twilight's glow, the world feels right,
Soft whispers of dusk weave through the trees,
A gentle hush carried by the breeze.

Shadows stretch long, as day meets night,
Painting our dreams in softest light,
In this quiet hour, moments collide,
With twilight's breath, we feel the tide.

Stars peek out, in the softening blue,
Each twinkle a promise, a glimpse of true,
Magic unfolds in the twilight's grace,
Time dances slowly in this sacred space.

Heartbeats align with the fading sun,
In twilight's embrace, the day is done,
Together we breathe in this soft caress,
Wrapped in the warmth of evening's dress.

Hold close the light as the shadows descend,
In this sacred hour, we mend and bend,
With twilight's gentle breath, we find our way,
To weave our dreams at the close of day.

A Ballet of Frost and Light

In the early morn, when the world's still dim,
A ballet unfolds on nature's whim,
Frosted petals dance in the sun's first beams,
Whirling and twirling in crystalline dreams.

Each blade of grass wears a sparkling crown,
Glittering treasures upon emerald gown,
In a delicate waltz, the shadows sway,
A ballet of frost as night turns to day.

The trees stand tall, their branches adorned,
With icy lace from the night they've mourned,
In harmony's grace, the cool winds might,
Lead us to places where warmth ignites.

Every glimmer a note in this symphony,
Nature's own music, wild and free,
With every heartbeat, a rhythm we find,
In a ballet of frost, our souls intertwined.

As the sun climbs high and the frost starts to fade,
The beauty remains in the light and shade,
Together we dance with the day taking flight,
In this grand performance of frost and light.

Silvery Echoes of the Night

Whispers dance in moonlight glow,
Shadows weave where secrets flow.
Stars above keep watchful eyes,
Dreams unfold beneath the skies.

Footsteps hush on velvet grass,
Time stands still, and moments pass.
Every sigh a fleeting sound,
Lost in night where peace is found.

Glimmers play on silver streams,
Softly float our silent dreams.
In the dark, the heart takes flight,
Finding solace in the night.

Fading echoes, tender grace,
Moonlit paths our steps embrace.
Every heartbeat, every breath,
A dance of life entwined with death.

As the night begins to wane,
Morning whispers of sweet pain.
Yet in silence, we'll reside,
In the echoes, love's our guide.

Chilling Reflections on Starlit Waters

Beneath the stars, the waters gleam,
Mirror worlds where shadows dream.
The cool night air, a whispered sigh,
Ripples form as secrets fly.

Pale lights touch the glassy surface,
Rippling tales we cannot trace.
Each glint a piece of stories told,
In moonlit hues, both shy and bold.

The water's edge, a quiet muse,
Silent thoughts we gently choose.
Every splash a fleeting fate,
Caught within the hands of late.

Time moves slow 'neath twinkling skies,
Every glance, a soft surprise.
Haunting echoes of the night,
In stillness found, a pure delight.

As dawn approaches with soft breath,
We bid goodbye, defying death.
Yet in reflections, we remain,
Forever caught in joy and pain.

The Calm Before the Dawn

A hush envelops all around,
Where whispers of the night abound.
Stars begin to fade away,
As shadows yield to break of day.

The world awaits in quiet grace,
While darkness clings to every space.
Soft light creeps on velvet skies,
A promise born where silence lies.

Birdsong teases, slow and sweet,
Nature stirs, feels the heartbeat.
Breath of morn, a gentle sweep,
Sings of dreams still held in sleep.

In this moment, time stands still,
Every heart, a silent thrill.
Nature's canvas painted bright,
Whispers of the coming light.

Awakening the world anew,
In hues of gold and softest blue.
The calm before the day begins,
Where hope ignites, and peace rescinds.

Mysteries Wrapped in Blue

Deep azure skies hold secrets tight,
Painting dreams with shades of night.
Waves of whispers, soft and true,
Unravel tales wrapped in the blue.

Every breath feels like a spell,
In the depths where echoes dwell.
A gentle tide, a sighing breeze,
Mysteries weave through changing seas.

Stars like diamonds, scattered bright,
Illuminate the canvas of night.
Where shadows whisper tales of old,
In hues of deep, a life unfolds.

Beneath the waves, where silence sings,
Secrets bound with silver strings.
In twilight's arms, we'll find our fate,
Wrapped in blue, we patiently wait.

As dawn approaches, painting skies,
We hold the deep with hopeful eyes.
For in the blue, the world is wide,
And in its depths, our hearts reside.

Fractal Night

In shadows deep, the fractals dance,
Infinity spins in a silent trance.
Stars flicker bright, in patterns they weave,
A universe formed, in dreams we believe.

Whispers of light, through the void they soar,
Each twinkle a story, a myth of yore.
Broken and whole, the night takes its flight,
In colors of chaos, a breathtaking sight.

Mirrors of time, reflecting our fears,
Fragments of laughter, and echoes of tears.
In the cosmic embrace, we find our delight,
Lost in the rhythms of fractal night.

Boundless horizons, where galaxies bend,
A waltz of the cosmos, with no clear end.
Together we float, in cosmic delight,
As dreams intertwine in the fractal night.

With every heartbeat, a pattern unfolds,
The tapestry rich, in silver and gold.
We drift amidst, the divine starlight,
Wrapped in the magic of fractal night.

Cosmic Silence

In the void, there's a whispering might,
A hush where dreams take their flight.
Stars hold their breath, in frozen grace,
In cosmic silence, we find our place.

Galaxies twirl in a quiet embrace,
Time itself slows, in this sacred space.
Nebulas blush, in shades of the night,
Painting the darkness with colors so bright.

Echoes of stardust linger and glide,
As the universe breathes, with nothing to hide.
The stillness of air, a soft lullaby,
In cosmic silence, where dreams softly lie.

Waves of creation, a delicate flow,
In the grandeur of nothing, we start to grow.
Silent reflections in the endless expanse,
Lost in the rhythm of a celestial dance.

From the depths of space to the heart of the mind,
A journey of solace, where we unbind.
Embracing the beauty of night's gentle sigh,
In cosmic silence, our spirits can fly.

Serene Shivers

A gentle breeze whispers through the trees,
Carrying secrets, soft as a tease.
Moonlight cascades in a silvery stream,
Filling the night with a serene dream.

In the quiet moments, a shiver ignites,
Soft shadows dance under starry lights.
Tucked in the arms of the silent night,
We find our solace, wrapped up tight.

The world fades away, in this tranquil place,
Each heartbeat echoes, an intimate grace.
Leaves rustle lightly, stories unfold,
A narrative whispered, in twilight's hold.

Pale glimmers of hope, in the chilly air,
The magic of night draws us to care.
Nature's embrace in a tender view,
Serene shivers wash over, anew.

Beneath the canopy of infinite skies,
We awaken to wonder, with unclouded eyes.
In the stillness, our souls gently quiver,
Basking in joy, with each serene shiver.

Frozen Echoes

In winter's grasp, the world holds its breath,
A shroud of white blankets, life and death.
Soft whispers linger in crystalline air,
Frozen echoes dance, unaware and bare.

Each flake that falls tells a story untold,
In silence profound, the night is bold.
Moonlight reflects on the shimmering ground,
Where frozen echoes of memories abound.

Time stands still, in this cold embrace,
Nature's pure canvas, a delicate space.
The heart beats slowly, with soft reprieve,
In the frozen stillness, we learn to believe.

Footprints of time in a powdery field,
Each step we take, a memory sealed.
The chill in the air is a tender kiss,
A moment suspended, a glimpse of bliss.

As dawn creeps in, with colors so rare,
The frozen echoes linger, aware.
We walk on the ice, where dreams intertwine,
In the beauty of stillness, our spirits align.

Timeless Winter's Kiss

Whispers of frost in the air,
Silent nights, a gentle stare.
Snowflakes dance, the world so still,
Wrapped in dreams, time cannot kill.

Moonlight paints the mountains white,
Stars above, a shimmering sight.
Branches bow with jeweled grace,
Winter's breath, a soft embrace.

Echoes of laughter in the chill,
Hearts aglow with warmth and thrill.
In the stillness, time unwinds,
Memories drift on winter winds.

Fires crackle, tales are spun,
In the hearth, our souls are one.
Underneath the snowy crest,
Winter's kiss, a treasured rest.

As the dawn breaks, gold and gray,
The world awakens to the day.
With every breath, a moment dear,
Timeless whispers, crystal clear.

Glacial Reflections

In the stillness of the night,
Icicles glint in silver light.
Frozen rivers gently flow,
Reflections dance, a luminous glow.

Mountains rise with sheets of white,
A canvas veiled, pure and bright.
Whispers echo through the vale,
Nature's song, a haunting tale.

Clouds embrace the peaks with grace,
Time slows down in this cold space.
Every breath a sigh, a plea,
In this world, just you and me.

Shimmering skies, a subtle hue,
Echoing dreams held close and true.
Stepping lightly on the ice,
Life is fleeting, oh so nice.

Stars above, a glimmering sea,
Casting light, setting spirits free.
In these glacial moments, find,
Reflections whisper, intertwined.

Celestial Harmony

In the vastness of the night,
Stars align in pure delight.
Twinkling lights, a cosmic dance,
In their glow, the heart's romance.

Waves of color, soft and bright,
Painting dreams in silver light.
Galaxies swirl, a waltz so grand,
Holding truths we cannot understand.

Moonbeams touch the earth so soft,
Lifting souls, they rise aloft.
Every twinkle tells a tale,
In celestial winds, we set sail.

Harmony of space and time,
Cosmic whispers, gentle rhyme.
In the silence, hearts unite,
A symphony of purest light.

Together, under stars we gaze,
Lost in the constants, time decays.
In this moment, all is clear,
Celestial love, forever near.

Distant Gleams

Over hills where shadows rest,
Distant gleams are nature's best.
Softly glowing through the trees,
Hints of gold on summer breeze.

Fields of green, a vibrant scene,
Dancing light, a perfect sheen.
As the sun dips, colors blend,
Painting skies that never end.

In the twilight, dreams take flight,
Chasing stars that gleam at night.
Heartbeats echo through the dark,
With every spark, a hidden mark.

Whispers carried on the wind,
Life's sweet stories softly pinned.
In the distance, hope ignites,
Guiding souls through endless nights.

Distant gleams, a call so near,
Embrace the journey, cast your fear.
Every step, a path we tread,
Chasing dawn where dreams are fed.

Evening's Spark

As sun dips low, the shadows grow,
Soft whispers dance in twilight's glow.
Stars awaken in the dusky sky,
Embers of dreams begin to fly.

A gentle breeze sways the trees,
Hushed secrets carried with ease.
Crickets sing their lullaby,
Underneath the fading sigh.

The world transforms in muted hues,
With every color, a different muse.
Evening's charm, a tender art,
Ignites the magic in the heart.

Within the stillness, whispers bloom,
Creating stories from the gloom.
Each sparkle paints a fleeting thought,
In the canvas night, we're caught.

As darkness falls, we gather round,
In shared silence, peace is found.
Evening's spark, a fleeting grace,
Inviting dreams to find their place.

Moonlit Reveries

Beneath the glow of silver light,
The world transforms into pure delight.
Shadows play on the soft, damp ground,
In the stillness, magic is found.

Whispers of the night softly call,
Echoing gently through the hall.
Moonlit paths of soft, glowing stones,
Lead us to places where spirit roams.

Clouds drift by, a silken shroud,
Veiling dreams that float on a cloud.
Stars twinkle like secrets untold,
In this dance, we are bold.

Time seems to pause in the night air,
Lost in reveries, free from care.
With every heartbeat, magic flows,
Under the witness of the moon's glows.

Mysteries weave through shadows deep,
In the silence, all awaken from sleep.
Moonlit reveries etch our soul,
Part of a larger, timeless whole.

Ghosts of the Constellations

Above us hangs a celestial sea,
Where constellations whisper to me.
Ghosts of stories lost in time,
Twinkle bright in a cosmic rhyme.

Faded legends drift like mist,
In a tapestry of stars, we exist.
Each point of light a tale to tell,
Of heroes, lovers, and places fell.

Navigating paths through starry night,
Guided by their gentle light.
Orion strides with sword in hand,
While Cassiopeia takes her stand.

Lost in reverie among the spheres,
Whispers echo, calming fears.
Ghostly shadows of ages past,
In this vast expanse, our dreams cast.

The sky a canvas, dark and wide,
Where memories and starlight abide.
Ghosts of the constellations speak,
In every glance, their tales unique.

The Quiet Dancer in the Night

In shadows deep, she starts to sway,
A quiet dancer at the end of day.
Graceful movements, soft and light,
Awakening dreams in the still of night.

Each twirl reveals a hidden grace,
As moonbeams kiss her gentle face.
The night embraces her jeweled heart,
In the silence, she plays her part.

The stars above begin to hum,
A melody from which dreams come.
Her steps weave stories of joy and pain,
Echoing softly like gentle rain.

The world watches as she twirls,
In the quiet, the night unfurls.
A tempest of calm envelops the air,
In her dance, we find our share.

She fades with dawn, a fleeting shadow,
Yet in our hearts, her spirit will flow.
The quiet dancer in the night,
Leaves us dreaming of her light.

Gentle Touch of the Moon's Breath

The silver glow on tranquil seas,
Whispers soft through swaying trees.
Stars like fireflies dance and gleam,
In the night's quiet, we dare to dream.

A breeze flows gently, calm and light,
With shadows playing, soft and bright.
Each wave a sigh, each tide a song,
In moon's embrace, we all belong.

The world stands still, held in this grace,
As time unfurls, a slow embrace.
Underneath the celestial dome,
The heart finds peace, the soul its home.

Between the clouds, a soft ray beams,
Guiding us through our sweetest dreams.
In this moment, fears take flight,
Wrapped in the moon's soft, tender light.

The night remembers, the stars conspire,
To spark our hearts, ignite desire.
With every breath, the magic flows,
In moonlit paths, love always grows.

Hushed Murmurs of an Ancient Sky

Beneath the vast and velvet night,
Whispers echo, lost in flight.
Stories woven through the air,
Of stardust dreams and cosmic fare.

Each twinkle holds a voice so wise,
Reflections of the bygone skies.
The legends swirl in twilight's glow,
In every heartbeat, they softly flow.

Like shadows cast by fading light,
The whispers dance, a delicate sight.
They tell of ages, trials and peace,
In the silence, mysteries cease.

Clouds gather close, a shroud of dreams,
As the moon hums tender themes.
The universe, a gentle muse,
Playing chords that hearts can use.

In this canvas, vast and grand,
We find our place, we understand.
With each sigh, the night takes hold,
Ancient tales in whispers told.

The Breath of Night's Chill

A crisp embrace surrounds the night,
As shadows stretch in silver light.
The world exhales, a breath so deep,
While dreams emerge from slumber's keep.

Frosted air, a gentle sigh,
Silhouettes glide beneath the sky.
The stars, like diamonds, pierce the dark,
Igniting hearts with a tiny spark.

In the stillness, secrets weave,
And time himself begins to leave.
Each frozen breeze carries a tale,
Of endless journeys, of ships that sail.

With every chill, the night unfolds,
Revealing wonders yet untold.
The moonlight dances, shadows twirl,
A ballet set in a starry whirl.

The breath of night, a spell so tight,
Holding hopes till morning light.
In its embrace, we find our peace,
A tranquil moment that will not cease.

Light and Ice

In winter's grip, where shadows lie,
Sunlight flickers, painting the sky.
Icicles hang like glassy tears,
Reflecting warmth, defying fears.

A dance of frost on windowpane,
Delicate patterns, a fleeting chain.
Each breath a cloud, soft and white,
Merging warmth with the chill of night.

In stillness, light begins to break,
Casting shadows, a subtle quake.
The world awakens, but remains still,
In harmony, with nature's will.

Tales of warmth in the frosty air,
Gentle kisses that linger there.
In moments carved by ice and glow,
We find the magic buried below.

As day unfolds, the ice will gleam,
A fleeting glimpse of a waking dream.
In unity, light and ice entwine,
Reminding us, life is divine.

Dreamscape of Snowlight

In silence deep where shadows play,
The snowflakes dance, a white ballet,
Whispers glide on frosty air,
A dreamscape woven with tender care.

Starlit paths in moonlit glow,
Guide the heart where wishes flow,
Each crystal spark, a story spun,
In winter's realm, we come undone.

Beneath the weight of softest white,
The world transforms in pure delight,
As branches bow in pure embrace,
In this enchanted, quiet space.

Hold close the warmth, the hearth's sweet light,
As we explore this tranquil night,
With every step, let worries cease,
In snowlight's dream, we find our peace.

And when the dawn begins to break,
Revelations form in every flake,
For in this dreamscape, magic thrives,
In snowlit whispers, our spirit dives.

Hush of Midnight

When night descends with velvet grace,
The world is wrapped in still embrace,
Stars flicker like a distant sigh,
A lullaby beneath the sky.

Silence sings with gentle ease,
As shadows dance among the trees,
Each breath a whisper, soft and clear,
In midnight's hush, we draw them near.

The moonlight weaves a silver thread,
Through dreams that linger, softly spread,
A tapestry of whispers faint,
In shadows deep, the heart can paint.

With every heartbeat, time stands still,
In the embrace of night, we fill,
Our souls with dreams, both wild and free,
In this enchanting reverie.

As dawn approaches, slowly bright,
We'll hold this hush, this sacred night,
For in the stillness, peace we find,
In hush of midnight, hearts aligned.

Chilled Stardust

In twilight's grasp, the stardust gleams,
A chilled embrace of whispered dreams,
Each spark a wish upon the air,
In this still night, a cosmic prayer.

The universe in silence hums,
As every heartbeat gently drums,
With every glance, the heavens sway,
In chilled stardust, we drift away.

With every breath, the cold ignites,
A symphony of shimmering lights,
In twilight's dance, our spirits roam,
Through galaxies, we find our home.

And as we wander, hand in hand,
Across the vast and starry land,
We'll trace the paths of dreams anew,
In chilled stardust, we break through.

So let the night embrace our souls,
As time demands and magic calls,
In every twinkle, let us trust,
In chilled stardust, wanderlust.

Frosted Nocturne

As night enfolds with frosted breath,
A symphony that dreams of death,
With every note, the cold descends,
In frosted nocturne, stillness bends.

The trees are cloaked in icy lace,
While moonlight carves the shadows' space,
Each whisper floats on frosty air,
A melody that lingers there.

In glimmering realms where wonders blend,
The stars respond, like faithful friends,
Together, we compose the night,
With every chord, a spark of light.

Embrace the chill, let worries fade,
In this nocturne, dreams are made,
With every sigh, the shadows sway,
In frosted notes, we find our way.

And when the dawn begins to glow,
We'll hold the night, a cherished show,
For in each song, our spirits yearn,
In frosted nocturne, we return.

Melodies of the Frozen Night

Whispers of cold dance in the air,
Underneath the shimmering glare.
Frozen breath upon the night,
Lending shadows their delicate light.

Stars twinkle like forgotten dreams,
Echoing soft, faint, silver beams.
Branches sigh, heavy with frost,
In this moment, nothing is lost.

A melody drifts through the trees,
Carried softly on the winter breeze.
Snowflakes fall like notes from above,
Creating a harmony we all love.

The world holds its breath in peace,
As the sounds of the night never cease.
Nature sings a lullaby true,
In the beauty of cold's gentle view.

Frigid nights hold stories untold,
In the silence, the ancient, the bold.
Every whisper, a tale from the past,
In the frozen night, moments cast.

Secrets of the Embracing Moon

Beneath the glow of silver hue,
The secrets of the night come through.
Stars align in patterns bright,
As the moon guards the shadows of light.

Whispers wander through the trees,
Carried gently on the breeze.
Soft sighs from the earth below,
Reveal the tales the night bestows.

Hidden lovers beneath the sky,
Exchanging dreams, a tender sigh.
In the moonlight, hearts entwine,
Bound together, a love divine.

Clouds drift lazily, a shroud of white,
Hiding stars from the watchful night.
Yet the moon, with its guiding grace,
Creates a bridge to an endless space.

Every shadow, a lover's plight,
Bathed in the warmth of the moon's light.
Secrets linger, softly spoken,
In each heartbeat, a love unbroken.

Symphony of Stars and Silence

In the hush of dusk's embrace,
Stars emerge with gentle grace.
A symphony begins to play,
In the night's enchanted ballet.

Faint echoes of a cosmic song,
Carried where the dreams belong.
Silence reigns in the velvet sky,
As the universe breathes a sigh.

Constellations weave stories grand,
Guiding travelers through the land.
Every twinkle, a whispered thought,
In this realm where peace is sought.

Galaxies swirl in cosmic dance,
Inviting souls to take a chance.
Each flicker brings hope anew,
In the silence, dreams come true.

Time stands still beneath the stars,
Healing memories, mending scars.
This symphony, a sacred tune,
Binds us all beneath the moon.

Threads of Frost

Threads of frost adorn the trees,
Sparkling softly in the breeze.
Nature wears a crown so bright,
Weaving magic in the night.

Delicate patterns, finely spun,
Kissed by moonlight, gently done.
Each crystal tells a silent tale,
In this winter's wondrous veil.

Beneath the chill, the earth sleeps deep,
Wrapped in dreams that softly creep.
Every glimmer, a wish unvoiced,
In the cold, we find our choice.

Frosty whispers fill the air,
With tales of love, joy, and care.
The world transforms, a stunning sight,
In the embrace of silver light.

As dawn approaches, shadows flee,
Revealing warmth and mystery.
Yet a trace of frost remains,
In the heart, where magic gains.

Chilled Echoes of Celestial Melodies

Beneath the stars, a whisper clear,
Echoes of dreams that we hold dear.
The night unfolds its velvet hue,
While frozen winds sing soft and true.

In shadows deep where silence sleeps,
The heart of winter gently weeps.
Each note a trace of love's embrace,
In cosmic dance, we find our place.

As silver beams caress the snow,
The winter's kiss begins to flow.
With every breath, the chill ignites,
A symphony of starry nights.

Through frosty air, the echoes rise,
A bridge of sound to winter skies.
We listen close, the world awakes,
In chilled echoes, our spirit shakes.

In moonlit glow, the night reveals,
The magic in what winter feels.
With every heartbeat, time suspends,
In chilled echoes, our journey blends.

Luminescence in the Frosty Air

Beneath the moon, the crystals gleam,
A dance of light, a wintry dream.
Each flake that falls, a spark divine,
In every corner, stars align.

The night is bright, though chill prevails,
With frost that sings in gentle trails.
The sun may hide, but hope will shine,
In luminescence, hearts entwine.

Soft whispers ride the icy breeze,
As shadows dance among the trees.
The world aglow with silver threads,
In frosty air, no one dreads.

In silence deep, the peace unfolds,
Each breath of winter, stories told.
A tapestry of night so rare,
With luminescence in the air.

Gathered round, we share our tales,
Of journeys crossed, of distant trails.
In every laugh, the warmth we share,
Is luminescent in the frosty air.

Dance of the Winter Spirits

In twilight's glow, the spirits play,
With light and shadow, they sway.
Through drifts of snow, they weave their art,
A dance of joy, a stirring heart.

With laughter bright, they fill the night,
In frosty breath, they take their flight.
They twirl and spin, a silver show,
In winter's breath, their magic flows.

Each gust of wind, a gentle tease,
Inviting dreams on dusky breeze.
With twinkling eyes, they haunt the trees,
In whispers soft, a winter's ease.

As moonlight casts its shifting glow,
The winter spirits steal the show.
In melodies of ice and flame,
They draw us in, we feel the same.

With every step, a melody,
A dance that sets our spirits free.
As night unfolds, we can't resist,
The dance of spirits, a winter's tryst.

Dreams Adrift in Midnight Air

In twilight's hush, dreams softly soar,
Adrift in night, forevermore.
Each wish a star, a beacon bright,
In midnight air, we find our light.

With thoughts that drift like winter's sigh,
We close our eyes and learn to fly.
In realms of hope, where shadows blend,
Our dreams take shape, our souls ascend.

Through velvet skies, our spirits glide,
Where frozen secrets quietly bide.
The night unveils a magic rare,
In dreams adrift, we find our care.

With every breath, the world unfolds,
A tapestry of tales retold.
In layers deep, our hearts will dare,
To leap from dreams into the air.

So let us chase the dreams we seek,
In midnight air, we find our peak.
Embracing night, we learn to dare,
To wander freely, happy, rare.

Frosty Reverence

In the stillness of the night,
Snowflakes whisper soft and bright.
Each breath a cloud, the air so clean,
Nature wrapped in white serene.

Trees adorned with icy lace,
Moonlight glimmers, a ghostly trace.
Footprints crunch beneath the hush,
Time stands still in winter's rush.

Breath visible in the chill,
Hearts feel heavy, yet so still.
A hush that blankets every sound,
In this reverence, peace is found.

Stars above twinkle cold and clear,
A tapestry that draws you near.
Frosty air fills lungs with grace,
In this realm, we find our place.

Silent moments gently weave,
In the frost, we learn to believe.
Life's fleeting warmth so soft and sweet,
In frosty reverence, we meet.

Cosmic Stillness

Among the stars, a tranquil space,
Where time and light begin to chase.
Galaxies swirl in dreamy sighs,
In cosmic stillness, the spirit flies.

Planets hum their distant tunes,
In velvet skies beneath the moons.
Nebulae glow with hues so rare,
In silent wonders, we lay bare.

Vast voids whisper ancient tales,
Of cosmic winds and starlit trails.
A universe both grand and small,
In stillness, we feel the call.

Hearts float like comets through the night,
Searching for love, for warmth, for light.
Each heartbeat echoes through the dark,
In cosmic stillness, we find our spark.

Dreamers cast their thoughts so high,
Reaching for what is on the fly.
In the silence between each star,
Cosmic stillness is never far.

Echoes of the Night

Beneath the moon, shadows creep,
In the silence, memories sleep.
Whispers in the gentle breeze,
Call to mind forgotten pleas.

Footfalls lost in dusky trails,
Softly drifting like the sails.
Echoes blend with distant sighs,
In the night, where longing lies.

Stars like eyes that softly gleam,
Watch over every whispered dream.
In the dark, our secrets soar,
Echoes beckon us to explore.

Night birds call with haunting grace,
In shadows, we confront our place.
The world asleep, yet thoughts alight,
In echoes of the tranquil night.

Every heartbeat says a prayer,
In the stillness, find your share.
Listen close, the night will show,
Echoes guide us where to go.

Velvet Eclipse

Shadows stretch across the land,
As daylight wanes, we make our stand.
A velvet touch upon the skies,
Where evening's hush begins to rise.

Moonlight dances, soft and low,
In twilight's arms, the stars aglow.
Whispers blend with the evening breeze,
As shadows stretch beneath the trees.

A moment caught in time's embrace,
Light and dark begin to chase.
Fleeting beauty, rare and deep,
In velvet eclipse, the night will keep.

Dreams unfold in the dusky hue,
A world transformed, yet somehow new.
In the quiet, secrets untwine,
As velvet skies begin to shine.

Hold your breath and close your eyes,
Let the stillness fill the skies.
In this magic, softly laced,
A velvet eclipse, time is graced.

Twilight Whispers

Soft shadows stretch as daylight fades,
Whispers of night in gentle cascades.
Stars begin to blink, a silent embrace,
Twilight unfolds with its tender grace.

Crickets chirp in a harmonious choir,
While the cool breeze builds a soft fire.
Memories linger on a silver thread,
As dreams awaken, where once they tread.

A canvas painted in hues of deep blue,
Flecks of gold mingle, a dance so true.
The world slows down, the heart beats light,
In the magic of this fleeting night.

Moonbeams scatter like jewels on the ground,
In twilight's tender arms, love is found.
Every whisper carries a story untold,
In this gentle hour where hearts unfold.

Nature holds its breath in raptured delight,
As silhouettes merge with the coming night.
Twilight whispers secrets, soft and clear,
A serenade of dreams that draw near.

Moonlit Reverie

Underneath a blanket of sapphire skies,
The moon ascends, a beacon that flies.
Glistening waves dance upon the shore,
In this tranquil moment, we ask for more.

Flickering candles cast shimmering light,
Illuminating paths through the silent night.
Dreams take flight on the wings of the breeze,
In the realm of shadows, we find our ease.

Stars twinkle softly in a cosmic embrace,
Each one a wish hidden in time and space.
A reverie blooms in the cool, crisp air,
While secrets are whispered without a care.

As we wander through fields of silver grains,
The universe hums in sweet refrains.
Moments like these are treasures to keep,
In the moonlit magic, our hearts take a leap.

The soul dances lightly on this tranquil night,
Bathed in the glow of soft, silvery light.
Every sigh of the wind sings its song,
In this moonlit reverie, we feel we belong.

Frost-kissed Dreams

Morning dew glistens on blades of green,
A frost-kissed canvas where beauty is seen.
Each breath is a whisper, icy and clear,
In the heart of winter, magic draws near.

Treetops wear crowns of shimmering white,
Nature transformed in the soft morning light.
Footsteps leave prints in the fresh fallen snow,
Marking a journey where dreams freely flow.

The tranquil hush blankets all in its might,
As day breaks anew, chasing away night.
With every heartbeat, the world gently sighs,
In the glow of the dawn, where hope never dies.

Frost-kissed dreams linger just out of reach,
Lessons of patience that nature can teach.
In each glistening drop, a story unfolds,
Of seasons and cycles, of life manifold.

We find warmth in layers, both physical and near,
As hearts beat together, dissolving all fear.
Frost-kissed moments, so fleetingly sweet,
Remind us of treasures that life does repeat.

Celestial Serenade

Stars shimmer bright in a velvet embrace,
Whispers of heavens woven in lace.
Galaxies twirl in a cosmic dance,
Inviting us softly to take a chance.

Time slows down in this infinite space,
Where dreams intertwine and sorrows efface.
A serenade strums through the fabric of night,
In notes of stardust, pure and bright.

Comets trail fire, a celestial glow,
Painting the heavens with vibrant show.
With each passing moment, we rise and we fall,
In this cosmic symphony that beckons us all.

The universe hums a tune so divine,
Echoing softly through space and through time.
Each twinkle a promise, a story to share,
In the vastness above, love dances in air.

Celestial whispers bring solace and peace,
As worries dissolve, and our hearts find release.
Together we dream under moon and star,
In this serenade, no distance is far.

Cosmic Frost

In the hush of midnight's breath,
Stars shimmer like frozen dreams.
The universe draped in a veil,
Whispers of ancient cosmic themes.

Shadows dance on icy plains,
As galaxies swirl in a waltz.
Each crystal flake tells a tale,
Of time's soft, fleeting faults.

Beneath this vast celestial dome,
Our souls feel the fragile thread.
In silent awe, we find our place,
Where stardust melts and dreams are bred.

The frost glistens on the pines,
A tapestry of night's delight.
Each breath, a mist, a fleeting sign,
Of life embraced in silver light.

With hearts entwined in cosmic play,
We wander through this starlit sea.
In every chill, in every ray,
We find the warmth of eternity.

Enchanted by the Night Sky

The night unfolds a velvet cloak,
Sprinkled with glimmering charade.
Whispers of magic softly spoke,
As dreams begin to cascade.

Moonbeams waltz on gentle streams,
Kissing the earth with silver grace.
Underneath the starry beams,
We drift into a sacred space.

The constellations weave our fate,
Stories written in the dark.
With every twinkle, we relate,
To journeys sparked, igniting a spark.

A breeze carries secrets untold,
While shadows watch, vigilant and wise.
Nature's heartbeat, soft yet bold,
Calls us to look beyond the skies.

In each breath of night's embrace,
We find the universe aligns.
An enchantment we can't replace,
As stars align in cosmic signs.

Twinkling Secrets Beneath the Stars

Beneath the vast, unfolding night,
Secret whispers gently flow.
Twinkling gems in endless flight,
Reveal the mysteries we long to know.

With every glance, a story unfolds,
Of love, of loss, of dreams reborn.
In celestial tones, the heart holds,
A warmth that shields against the scorn.

The cosmos sings in gentle grace,
A melody born of ancient time.
In every flicker, a hidden place,
Where hope and wonder intertwine.

Each twinkle holds a secret glance,
An echo of what once was real.
In cosmic dance, we find our chance,
To touch the stars, our hearts to heal.

So let us wander in the dark,
Embracing what the night bestows.
Beneath the twinkling, we embark,
Towards dreams, as softly they compose.

Radiance in the Moon's Glow

Underneath the moon's embrace,
Shadows shimmer, softly dance.
Each beam a tender, glowing trace,
We lose ourselves in night's romance.

The silver light, a loving touch,
Wraps the world in whispers sweet.
In every corner, oh so much,
A tranquil heart, a rhythmic beat.

As night unveils its radiant charm,
The wilderness breathes in silent awe.
Calming fears, a soothing balm,
In moonlit dreams, we lose the flaw.

The stars twinkle in soft reply,
A tapestry of hope above.
Together we gaze, you and I,
In this celestial dance of love.

So let the moon light our escape,
Through realms of peace and quiet grace.
Wrapped in warmth, the night takes shape,
In the radiance we embrace.

Milton Keynes UK
Ingram Content Group UK Ltd.
UKHW010232111224
452348UK00011B/708